Holiday Cooking Made Easy

Thanksgiving and Christmas Recipes for Beginners

Les Ilagan

Copyright © CONTENT ARCADE PUBLISHING
All rights reserved.

This cookbook is copyright protected and meant for personal use only. No part of this cookbook may be used, paraphrased, reproduced, scanned, distributed or sold in any printed or electronic form without permission of the author and the publishing company. Copying pages or any part of this book for any purpose other than own personal use is prohibited and would also mean violation of copyright law.

DISCLAIMER

Content Arcade Publishing and its authors are joined together in their efforts in creating these pages and their publications. Content Arcade Publishing and its authors make no assurance of any kind, stated or implied, with respect to the information provided.

LIMITS OF LIABILITY

Content Arcade Publishing and its authors shall not be held legally responsible in the event of incidental or consequential damages in line with, or arising out of, the supplying of the information presented here.

Table of Contents

Introduction 1

Holiday Turkey with Maple and Herbs........................ 2

Perfect Stuffed Turkey 4

Roasted Honey Mustard Chicken............................... 7

Spicy Roasted Garlic Chicken 9

Grilled Steak with Spicy Cranberry Glaze.................. 11

Black Bean Turkey Chili Picadillo 13

Minced Beef Pasta and Mushroom Bake................... 15

Easy Peppered Roast Beef.. 17

Homemade Savory Meat Loaf 20

The Ultimate Meatloaf Recipe 22

Lasagna with Spinach Mushroom and Ricotta........... 24

Holiday Breakfast Frittata 26

Salmon with Mango-Avocado Salsa 28

Rosemary Meatloaf.. 30

Roasted Rib Eye and Vegetables 32

Farfalle with Roasted Vegetables 34

Spaghetti with Turkey Meatballs in.......................... 36

Tomato Sauce.. 36

Salmon Pasta and Broccoli Salad.............................. 38

Baked Cod Fillet with Stewed Pumpkin 40

- Chicken and Pumpkin Stew 42
- Pumpkin Zucchini and Chickpea Stew 44
- with Feta 44
- Spicy Beef and Pumpkin Stew 46
- Tex-Mex Turkey Soup 48
- Pumpkin Soup with Cheddar 50
- Cheesy Broccoli and Cherry Tomato Quiche 52
- Chicken Mushroom and Leek Quiche 54
- Chunky Chicken and Apple Salad 56
- Zucchini Tomato and Feta Salad 58
- Rocket Peach and Feta Salad 60
- Fresh Italian Garden Salad 62
- Red Cabbage Slaw with Pomegranates 64
- Chicken Macaroni Salad with Mixed Veggies 66
- Zucchini Muffins with Turkey Ham 68
- Cheesy Mini Mediterranean Pizza 70
- Vegetable and Cheddar Kebabs 72
- Homemade Gingerbread Cookies 73
- Easy Sugar Cookies 75
- Holiday Chocolate Chip Cookies 77
- Peanut Butter Christmas Cookies 79
- Holiday Molasses Cookies 81
- Bread Pudding with Dried Cranberries 83

Spiced Almond Pumpkin Waffles 85
Carrot Walnut Cupcake with Cinnamon...................... 87
Honey Cake with Walnuts... 90
Pumpkin Muffin with Whipped Cream Topping 92
Cinnamon Rolls with Dried Cherries and Almonds 94
Traditional Pecan Pie with Maple Syrup 96
Homemade Scones with Chocolate Chips.................. 98
and Walnuts.. 98
Fresh Peach Pie Home-Style 100
Rustic Apple Pie Home-Style...................................102
Luscious Cranberry Pie..104
Orange Pumpkin Pie 106
Apple Pie Ala Mode...108
Turtle Pie Cheesecake with Pecans..........................110
Spiced Pumpkin Cheesecake...................................112
Cherry Pie with Rhubarb and Honey........................114
Carrot Cake with Prunes and Walnuts......................116
Baked Apples with Raisins and Pecans.....................118
Crème Brulee Home-Style 120
Blueberry Pecan Cheesecake in a Jar.......................122
Raspberry Kiwi and Pineapple Skewers....................124
Holiday Fruit Kebabs...125
Sugar-Coated Cranberries 126

Pecan Tarts with Maple 127

Homemade Port Cranberry Sauce........................... 129

Christmas Hot Chocolate with Mallows.................... 131

Spiced Hot Chocolate with Nutella 133

Hot Chocolate with Cinnamon 135

Spiced Egg Nog 137

Holiday Irish Coffee 139

Hot Apple Cider 140

Introduction

The "Holidays" is the best time to be merry and thankful for all the blessings that we have received. We would always want to make sure to celebrate them with our dear family and friends.

Any festivity won't be complete without sharing sumptuous food and drinks on the table with our loved ones. This book will give you many wonderful ideas on what to serve for the holidays.

Just a tip, if you are hosting a dinner party, it is always best to plan your menu in advance so that you'll have a stress-free holiday.

Whether you are serving meals for the family or to a larger group, you will surely find here the perfect recipes that you can serve for them. It is packed with wonderful Holiday recipes which are made simple that even those new to cooking can easily follow. From traditional to modern takes on classic recipes, this book has it all.

It is a part of many cookbook series that I am writing, I hope you'll enjoy reading and trying out all the recipes in this book.

So now, let's get started!

Holiday Turkey with Maple and Herbs

Preparation Time: 30 minutes
Total Time: 4 hours 30 minutes
Yield: 24 servings

Ingredients

2 cups apple cider vinegar
1/3 cup real maple syrup
3 Tbsp. fresh rosemary (chopped)
3 Tbsp. fresh thyme (chopped)
2 1/2 tsp. grated lemon zest
3/4 cup butter (softened)
14 pounds whole turkey
2 medium onion (chopped)
2 celery stalks (diced)
2 medium carrot (diced)
salt and freshly ground black pepper

Method

1. Combine apple cider and maple syrup in a heavy saucepan and boil over medium-high heat for 20 minutes, it should be reduced to a 1/2 cup. Remove from heat. Stir in 1/2 of the thyme and marjoram and the 2 1/2 teaspoon lemon zest. Add the ¾ cup of butter, and mix well until melted. Season to taste. Transfer to a small glass bowl, let cool, and then cover with plastic wrap. Refrigerate until cold.

2. Preheat your oven to 375 F. Place the oven rack in the lowest third of your oven.
3. Rinse and pat dry turkey, and place in a large baking dish. Loosen the turkey skin by sliding hand under it. Gently rub 1/2 cup of the maple butter mixture under the breast skin. Rub another 1/4 cup of the mixture over the outside of the turkey. Using a kitchen string, tie the legs of turkey together.
4. Place the carrot, celery, and onion around the turkey in the baking dish. Sprinkle the remaining herbs over the vegetables, and add the chicken stock into the pan.
5. Cook turkey for 30 minutes in the preheated oven. Reduce oven temperature to 350 F, and cover turkey loosely with aluminum foil. Cook further 3-4 hours for unstuffed or 4-5 hours for stuffed. You will know if it's done if the internal temperature of the thigh reaches 180 F. Transfer turkey to a large serving platter, and tent with foil. Allow turkey to cool, about 20 minutes before carving.
6. Serve and enjoy.

Nutritional Information:
Energy - 287 calories
Fat - 12.1 g
Carbohydrates - 4.9 g
Protein - 36.9 g
Sodium - 232 mg

Perfect Stuffed Turkey

Preparation Time: 30 minutes
Total Time: 17 hours
Yield: 24 Servings

Ingredients:
1 medium sized whole turkey with skin
1/2 cup butter, softened

For the Brine:
2 cups kosher salt
1 ½ US gallon water

For the Stuffing:
2 large onions (peeled and diced)
4 carrots (peeled and diced)
4 stalks celery (finely chopped)
1/4 cup fresh thyme leaves (chopped)
1 bay leaf
4 whole fresh pimiento (chopped)
1 tsp. cumin seeds
1 tsp. ground black pepper
1 cup grape juice
1 Tbsp. lemon juice

For the Sauce:
4 cups turkey stock
1/2 oz. dried porcini mushrooms

1/4 cup butter
1/4 cup flour
1 tsp. vinegar
2 Tbsp. heavy cream
Salt and pepper

Method:
1. For the brine solution: in a large stockpot mix water, kosher salt and lemon together then set aside.
2. For the turkey: remove neck, giblets and liver from the turkey. Properly wash and clean it, then pat dry with paper towels.
3. Soak the turkey in brine solution, cover it with plastic cling wrap and refrigerate for about 12 hours or overnight.
4. Preheat the roaster oven to 450 F.
5. Remove the turkey from the refrigerator, set aside the brine solution as turkey stock and thoroughly rinse the turkey under cold water, pat it dry
6. Baste the turkey with melted butter and season it with pepper and cumin.
7. Stuff the cavity with onion, carrots, celery, thyme, bay leaf and fresh pimiento.
8. Place the turkey in insert pan of roaster oven - breast side down. Pour grape juice and lemon over it, and then roast at the highest setting for about 30 minutes.
9. After 30 minutes, reduce the temperature to 325 F and roast for about 20 minutes more. Again, reduce the temperature to 250F and roast for another 30 minutes.

10. Similarly, reduce the temperature after every 30-40 minutes until the final temperature comes out to be 180F. The total roasting time should not extend up to 4 hours.
11. Using a knife, check the doneness. Carefully wrap roasted turkey in aluminum foil and let it rest for 15 minutes at room temperature before serving.
12. For the sauce: boil mushrooms in the turkey stock for 15 minutes, then melt butter in a saucepan and fry the chopped boiled mushrooms for about 5 minutes. Whisk in flour and stir for about 2-3 minutes. Add the reserved turkey stock, salt and pepper in it and cook for 5 minutes, then add vinegar and heavy cream and let it simmer for 10 more minutes over medium low heat. Store inside the refrigerator.
13. Decorate the roasted turkey with the carrot spirals and sprinkle some chopped parsley.
14. Serve with porcini mushroom sauce.

Nutritional Information:

Energy - 325 calories
Fat - 14.1 g
Carbohydrates - 8.9 g
Protein - 38.9 g
Sodium - 310 mg

Roasted Honey Mustard Chicken

Preparation Time: 15 minutes
Total Time: 1 hour
Yield: 8 servings

Ingredients

1 (2.5 lbs.) whole chicken

salt and pepper to taste

1/2 cup honey

1/4 cup Dijon mustard

2 Tbsp. regular mustard

2 Tbsp. lime juice

2 Tbsp. fresh thyme (chopped)

2 Tbsp. fresh parsley (chopped)

2 cloves garlic (minced)

cooking oil spray

Method

1. Preheat your oven to 375 F.
2. Place chicken in a baking dish. Pat dry with paper towel and then season with salt and pepper to taste. Set aside.
3. Mix together the honey, Dijon mustard, regular mustard, lime juice, thyme, parsley, and garlic in a small bowl. Spoon half of the mixture over the chicken, and brush to coat evenly.
4. Bake in the oven for 30 minutes. Turn chicken over and brush the other side with the remaining honey

mustard mixture. Bake further 15 minutes, or until chicken is browned and the juices run clear. Remove from heat and allow to cool slightly, about 10 minutes before slicing.
5. Serve and enjoy.

Nutritional Information:
Energy - 290 calories
Fat - 6.6 g
Carbohydrates - 19.7 g
Protein - 37.4 g
Sodium - 243 mg

Spicy Roasted Garlic Chicken

Preparation Time: 20 minutes
Total Time: 1 hour
Yield: 4 servings

Ingredients

1/4 cup butter (melted)
1 tsp. onion powder
1 tsp. rosemary (dried)
1 tsp. paprika
1 tsp. cayenne pepper (ground)
1/2 tsp. Kosher salt
1/2 tsp. freshly ground black pepper
1 whole chicken (cut into quarters)
12 cloves garlic (thinly sliced)
cooking oil spray

Method

1. Preheat your oven to 400 F.
2. Place chicken pieces into a baking dish. Brush all sides generously with butter. Add garlic and set aside.
3. Combine the onion powder, rosemary, paprika, cayenne pepper, salt, and black pepper in a small bowl. Mix well.
4. Sprinkle spice mixture over chicken pieces coating evenly on both sides.
5. Place the baking dish into the preheated oven and cook chicken for about 40-45 minutes, or until juices

from the chicken run clear. Turning half-way through cooking.
6. Transfer to a serving dish.
7. Serve immediately and enjoy.

Nutritional Information:
Energy - 376 calories
Fat - 18.5 g
Carbohydrates - 4.4 g
Protein - 51.6 g
Sodium - 485 mg

Grilled Steak with Spicy Cranberry Glaze

Preparation Time: 15 minutes
Total Time: 2 hours 30 minutes
Yield: 8 servings

Ingredients

3 cloves garlic (minced)
1/2 tsp. Kosher salt
2 Tbsp. ketchup
2 Tbsp. olive oil
1/2 tsp. black pepper (ground)
1/2 tsp. oregano (dried)
2 lbs. flank steak
cooking oil spray

Spicy Cranberry Glaze:
2 Tbsp. butter
1 cup cranberry sauce
1/2 cup fresh orange juice
1 Tbsp. maple syrup
1 tsp. hot chili flakes
1/4 tsp. cinnamon (ground)

Method

1. Mix together garlic, salt, ketchup, olive oil, black pepper, and oregano in a small bowl.
2. Take the meat and score both sides (diamond cut), about 1/8 inch deep. Rub the prepared garlic mixture

into both sides of the steak. Cover tightly with plastic or cling wrap and then refrigerate for at least 4 hours.
3. Meanwhile, prepare the cranberry glaze by melting the butter in a small saucepan over medium heat. Stir in cranberry sauce, orange juice, maple syrup, and chili flakes. Cook for 3-5 minutes, stirring often. Remove from heat and set aside.
4. Preheat grill to high and lightly oil grate with oil spray.
5. Grill meat on the prepared grill. Cook for 7 minutes per side, or to your desired doneness. Cut into portions.
6. Transfer to individual serving dish and drizzle with spicy cranberry glaze.
7. Serve immediately and enjoy.

Nutritional Information:
Energy - 300 calories
Fat - 12.5 g
Carbohydrates - 5.8 g
Protein - 38.5 g
Sodium - 510 mg

Black Bean Turkey Chili Picadillo

Preparation Time: 15 minutes
Total Time: 40 minutes
Yield: 6 Servings

Ingredients:

For the Picadillo:
2 Tbsp. olive oil (divided)
16 oz. turkey meat (ground)
1 large yellow onion (finely chopped)
1 green bell pepper (finely chopped)
1 Tbsp. garlic paste
1 bay leaf
1/2 cup white grape juice
1/2 Tbsp. lemon juice
8 oz. fresh tomato paste
1/2 cup pimiento stuffed green olives (finely chopped)
1/3 cup raisins
1/2 cup boiled black beans
1 Tbsp. sliced olives in brine (drained)
1 Tbsp. capers
2 tsp. ground cumin
Cayenne pepper, to taste

For the beans:
1/2 cup black beans
Water
1 tsp. of baking soda

Method:
1. Soak the black beans in enough water and a teaspoon of baking soda for at least 12 hours or overnight.
2. Heat a tablespoon of olive oil in the pan, add in ground turkey meat and cook over medium heat for 10 minutes or until the meat is no longer pink.
3. Transfer to a bowl and set aside. Clean pan and heat 1 tablespoon of fresh oil over low heat then add in onions, bell pepper, garlic paste and a bay leaf and sauté for 5 minutes.
4. Stir in cooked ground turkey, grape juice, lemon juice, tomato paste, stuffed olives, raisins, black beans, olive brine, capers, cayenne, cumin and salt. Bring mixture to a boil and let it simmer over medium-low heat, about 25 minutes or until the beans get tender and creamy.
5. Add in water if required to achieve the desired consistency of the picadillo. Remove bay leaf before serving.
6. Pour into serving bowls, garnish with fresh parsley leaves.
7. Serve warm with brown rice.

Nutritional Information:

Energy - 338 calories

Fat – 14.7 g

Carbohydrates – 26.3 g

Protein – 24.6 g

Sodium - 687 mg

Minced Beef Pasta and Mushroom Bake

Preparation Time: 10 minutes
Total Time: 55 minutes
Yield: 8 servings

Ingredients

2 Tbsp. olive oil

1 medium onion (chopped)

3 cloves garlic (minced)

1 1/2 lbs. beef sirloin (ground)

1 cup cherry tomatoes (quartered)

2 cups tomato puree

1 cup button mushroom (sliced)

1 medium red bell pepper (diced)

2 Tbsp. tomato paste

1 tsp. sweet paprika

1/2 tsp. sage (dried)

1/2 tsp. thyme (dried)

1/2 tsp. Kosher salt

1/2 tsp. freshly ground black pepper

4 cups cooked macaroni

1/2 cup cheddar cheese

1/4 cup parmesan cheese

Method

1. Heat 2 tablespoons olive oil in a large pot or saucepan over medium-high flame. Stir-fry onion for 3 minutes or until translucent.
2. Add the beef and cook for 7 minutes, or until browned.
3. Add the cherry tomatoes, tomato puree, bell pepper, tomato paste, paprika, sage, and thyme. Simmer for 15 minutes, stirring often. Season to taste.
4. Add the cooked pasta and stir to combine well. Remove from heat.
5. Transfer to a baking dish. Sprinkle with cheddar and parmesan cheese.
6. Bake in the oven for 10 minutes. Cool slightly.
7. Serve immediately and enjoy.

Nutritional Information:
Energy - 387 calories
Fat - 12.5 g
Carbohydrates - 34.1 g
Protein - 34.5 g
Sodium - 297 mg

Easy Peppered Roast Beef

Preparation Time: 15 minutes
Total Time: 1 hour
Yield: 10 servings

Ingredients

1 ½ Tbsp. garlic (chopped)
1 tsp. Kosher salt (divided)
3 Tbsp. olive oil
2 1/2 lbs. beef tri-tip roast (trimmed)
1 Tbsp. fresh thyme (chopped)
1 Tbsp. fresh rosemary (chopped)
1 Tbsp. whole black peppercorns (coarsely ground)
1 Tbsp. whole white peppercorns (coarsely ground)
2 Tbsp. unsalted butter

Sauce:
1 1/3 Tbsp. all-purpose flour
1 cup beef stock (reduced sodium)
2 Tbsp. red wine vinegar
1 Tbsp. Worcestershire sauce
salt and freshly ground black pepper

Method

1. Place garlic and some salt into a mortar and pestle. Crush and grind until it forms a paste. Stir in olive oil into garlic mixture.

2. Place beef into a baking dish and brush with prepared garlic paste on both sides of the roast. Season with kosher salt.
3. Combine the herbs and peppercorns in a small bowl.
4. Melt butter in a large ovenproof pan. Turn off the heat.
5. Place beef into the baking dish and brush both sides with butter.
6. Press the herb-peppercorn mixture onto the beef and coat generously.
7. Preheat your oven to 450 F.
8. Roast meat in the oven for about 15 minutes. Take out from the oven and turn to cook the other side. Lower oven temperature to 200 F. Cook for another 15 minutes or until an instant-read meat thermometer, inserted into the middle of the roast, is showing 130 F.
9. Place roast beef to a platter and cover loosely with aluminum foil. Cool slightly for 10-15 minutes.
10. Meanwhile, prepare the sauce. In a small saucepan combine the pan juices, beef stock, flour, red wine vinegar, and Worcestershire sauce. Mix well, it should be free from lumps. Bring to a boil, stirring often. Lower heat and cook further 3 minutes or until thickened, stirring frequently. Transfer to a serving dish.
11. Carve the roast beef across the grain.
12. Serve slices on individual plates drizzled with prepared sauce.
13. Enjoy.

Nutritional Information:
Energy - 271 calories
Fat - 12.4 g
Carbohydrates - 3.0 g
Protein - 35.1 g
Sodium - 420 mg

Homemade Savory Meat Loaf

Preparation Time: 10 minutes
Total Time: 1 hour 10 minutes
Yield: 10 servings

Ingredients

2 lbs. beef sirloin (ground)
1 medium onion (chopped)
1 large egg
1 cup whole milk
1 cup breadcrumbs (dry)
salt and freshly ground black pepper
1/3 cup ketchup
2 Tbsp. brown sugar
2 Tbsp. Dijon mustard

Method

1. Preheat your oven to 350 F.
2. In a large bowl, combine the meat, onion, egg, milk and breadcrumbs. Add some salt and pepper to taste and transfer into a lightly greased 5x9 inch loaf pan. Set aside.
3. Mix together the ketchup, brown sugar, and Dijon mustard in a small bowl. Pour over the meatloaf.
4. Place in the preheated oven and bake for 1 hour. Let cool before cutting into portions.
5. Serve and enjoy.

Nutritional Information:
Energy - 271 calories
Fat - 8.2 g
Carbohydrates - 13.9 g
Protein - 33.6 g
Sodium - 345 mg

The Ultimate Meatloaf Recipe

Preparation Time: 15 minutes
Total Time: 1 hour 15 minutes
Yield: 10 servings

Ingredients

2 lbs. ground beef
1 cup breadcrumbs
1/2 cup diced green bell pepper
1 large onion (chopped)
1/2 cup milk
1/3 cup steak sauce
1 large egg
1 tsp. salt
1/4 tsp. freshly ground black pepper
cooking oil spray

Method

1. Preheat your oven to 350 F. Lightly grease an 8 1/2 x 4 1/2 inch loaf pan with oil spray.
2. Mix together the meat, bread crumbs, bell pepper, onion, milk, and half of the steak sauce. Season to taste.
3. Transfer the mixture into the prepared loaf pan and smoothen the top, pressing gently. Brush with the remaining steak sauce.
4. Bake in the preheated oven for about an hour or until done. Cool slightly before slicing.

5. Transfer to a serving dish.
6. Serve and enjoy.

Nutritional Information:
Energy - 253 calories
Fat - 8.4 g
Carbohydrates - 12.1 g
Protein - 30.2 g
Sodium - 450 mg

Lasagna with Spinach Mushroom and Ricotta

Preparation Time: 35 minutes
Total Time: 1 hour 50 minutes
Yield: 12 servings

Ingredients

15 dry lasagna noodles

2 Tbsp. olive oil

1 cup onion (chopped)

1 Tbsp. garlic (minced)

2 cups fresh mushrooms (chopped)

2 cups fresh spinach

2 cups ricotta cheese

1/2 cup grated Romano cheese

1 tsp. Kosher salt

1 tsp. oregano (dried)

1 tsp. basil leaves (dried)

1/2 tsp. ground black pepper

1 whole egg (beaten)

3 cups tomato sauce

1 cup mozzarella cheese (shredded)

3/4 cup Parmesan cheese (grated)

Method

1. Preheat your oven to 350 F.
2. Bring a large stockpot of lightly salted water to a boil. Add the lasagna noodles. Cook for like 10-12 minutes or until the pasta is al dente. Drain.

3. In a skillet over medium-high heat, heat olive oil and stir fry onion and garlic for 3 minutes.
4. Add mushrooms. Cook for 5 minutes, stirring occasionally. Remove from heat.
5. Boil spinach for 3-5 minutes. Drain, allow to cool and then squeeze out excess liquid. Chop the spinach.
6. In a large bowl, combine the ricotta cheese, Romano cheese, sautéed mushrooms, spinach, salt, oregano, basil, pepper, and egg. Mix well.
7. Lay 5 lasagna noodles in bottom of a 9x13 inch baking dish. Spread one third of the ricotta-spinach mixture over pasta. Sprinkle 1/3 cup mozzarella cheese and 1/4 cup Parmesan cheese on top. Spread 1 cup tomato sauce over cheese. Repeat procedure for next 2 layers.
8. Cover baking dish with aluminum foil. Bake in the oven for 1 hour. Allow lasagne to cool for a few minutes before serving.
9. Serve and enjoy.

Nutritional Information:
Energy - 432 calories
Fat - 9.2 g
Carbohydrates - 69.4 g
Protein - 20.4 g
Sodium - 665 mg

Holiday Breakfast Frittata

Preparation Time: 10 minutes
Total Time: 30 minutes
Yield: 4 servings

Ingredients

2 Tbsp. olive oil
3 cups kale (chopped)
1/2 medium yellow onion (sliced)
1 cup sliced mushrooms (like oyster or button mushrooms)
2 garlic cloves (minced)
2 oz. deli turkey ham (chopped)
6 whole eggs
1/4 cup milk
1 tsp. dried thyme (chopped)
Salt and pepper

Method

1. Preheat oven to 350F.
2. Heat the olive oil in an oven-proof pan or cast iron skillet.
3. Add the chopped kale and onions. Cook for 5 minutes. Add the mushrooms and garlic. Cook for 3-4 minutes. Stir in the chopped turkey ham and remove from the heat.
4. In a bowl beat the eggs, milk, thyme, salt, and pepper. Pour the eggs over vegetable mixture and do

not stir. Place the cast iron skillet into preheated oven.
5. Bake the frittata for 20 minutes or until the eggs are set.
6. Remove from the oven and cut into wedges. Serve and enjoy.

Nutritional Information:
Energy - 207 calories
Fat - 10.1 g
Carbohydrates - 5.9 g
Protein - 29.9 g
Sodium - 255 mg

Salmon with Mango-Avocado Salsa

Preparation Time: 15 minutes
Total Time: 20 minutes
Yield: 4 servings

Ingredients

1 Tbsp. smoked paprika
1/2 Tbsp. cayenne pepper
4 thyme springs (leaves only)
salt and pepper
4 (5 oz.) wild salmon steak
1 Tbsp. olive oil

Mango-avocado salsa:
1 ripe mango (peeled, deseeded and cubed)
1 large avocado (peeled and cubed)
2 Tbsp. fresh cilantro (chopped)
2 Tbsp. lemon juice
1 Tbsp. olive oil

Method

1. Prepare the mango-avocado salsa by mixing all the ingredients thoroughly in a medium bowl. Season to taste and then keep refrigerated until ready to use.
2. Combine smoked paprika, cayenne pepper, thyme and salt and pepper in food processor; pulse until well combined.

3. Transfer into shallow dish and coat salmon well with the mixture.
4. Heat oil in large non-stick skillet and when heated add the salmon fillets.
5. Cook salmon 4-5 minutes, each side, flipping carefully.
6. Serve while still hot and top with chilled salsa.

Nutritional Information:
Energy - 359 calories
Fat - 24.1 g
Carbohydrates – 15.2 g
Protein – 23.9 g
Sodium – 256 mg

Rosemary Meatloaf

Preparation Time: 10 minutes
Total Time: 1 hour 10 minutes
Yield: 6 servings

Ingredients

1 1/2 lbs. ground beef

1/2 cup chopped onions

1 Tbsp. all-purpose flour

2 Tbsp. fresh chopped rosemary

2 garlic cloves, minced

1 whole egg, slightly beaten

1/3 cup tomato ketchup

2 Tbsp. apple puree

1 tsp. smoked paprika

1 ½ tsp. salt

1/2 tsp. freshly ground pepper

Method

1. Preheat oven to 350 F and grease meatloaf pan with oil spray.
2. Place all ingredients, except egg in a large bowl.
3. Stir well until combined and add egg.
4. Stir again until egg is well incorporated.
5. Transfer mixture to greased loaf pan.
6. Bake for 45 minutes and remove from the oven.
7. Place on wire rack to cool for 15 minutes before slicing.

Nutritional Information:
Energy - 249 calories
Fat - 8.1 g
Carbohydrates – 6.6 g
Protein – 36.0 g
Sodium - 610 mg

Roasted Rib Eye and Vegetables

Preparation Time: 20 minutes
Total Time: 2 hours
Yield: 8 servings

Ingredients

2 lbs. beef rib eye, boneless

1 Tbsp. dried sage

1 tsp. black pepper, cracked

2 Tbsp. mustard seeds

1/4 cup Dijon mustard

1/4 cup olive oil

1 stick butter, room temperature

1 tsp. Kosher salt

4 potatoes, peeled and cut into wedges

2 red bell peppers, halved

Method

1. Preheat oven to 480F.
2. Lightly crush the sage, pepper, mustard seeds, and salt using a mortar and pestle. Add some oil and pound until combined well.
3. In a separate bowl combine Dijon mustard and butter, until well mixed.
4. Brush the beef with oil mixture thoroughly and cook in heated large skillet, over medium-high heat for 3 minutes or until browned on each sides. Remove from the pan and secure with cooking string.

5. Rub the beef with prepared Dijon-butter mixture and place into a baking dish.
6. Add the potatoes and bell pepper.
7. Place in the oven and roast for about an hour.
8. Cover the meat with aluminum foil and let it rest for 10 minutes before slicing and serving.
9. Serve and enjoy.

Nutritional Information:
Energy - 249 calories
Fat - 8.1 g
Carbohydrates – 6.6 g
Protein – 36.0 g
Sodium - 610 mg

Farfalle with Roasted Vegetables

Preparation Time: 15 minutes
Total Time: 40 minutes
Yield: 4 servings

Ingredients

8 oz. farfalle or bow-tie pasta (dry)
2 cups cherry tomatoes (halved)
1 medium carrot (diced)
1 medium red bell pepper (diced)
1 medium green bell pepper (diced)
1/4 cup flat-leaf parsley (coarsely chopped)
2 Tbsp. olive oil
salt and freshly ground black pepper

Dressing:
1/4 cup olive oil
1/4 cup balsamic vinegar
1 Tbsp. honey
1/2 tsp. garlic powder
1/4 tsp. kosher salt
1/4 tsp. freshly ground black pepper

Method

1. Preheat your oven to 425 F.

2. In a stockpot over medium-high heat, cook pasta in lightly salted boiling water, following the package directions. Drain.
3. In a baking dish combine the cherry tomatoes, carrot, and bell peppers. Drizzle with some olive oil; season to taste.
4. Place in the oven and cook, uncovered, for about 20 minutes. Allow to cool.
5. Meanwhile, prepare dressing by whisking together the olive oil, balsamic vinegar, honey, garlic powder, salt, and pepper. Mix well. Set aside.
6. Place the pasta, roasted vegetables, parsley, and dressing into a large bowl. Toss to coat.
7. Transfer to individual serving plates.
8. Serve and enjoy.

Nutritional Information:
Energy - 375 calories
Fat - 21.1 g
Carbohydrates - 41.9 g
Protein - 7.4 g
Sodium - 323 mg

Spaghetti with Turkey Meatballs in Tomato Sauce

Preparation Time: 25 minutes
Total Time: 50 minutes
Yield: 6 servings

Ingredients

1 lb. spaghetti noodles (dry)
1 lb. turkey breast (ground)
1/2 cup breadcrumbs
1 medium egg
1/4 cup fresh parsley (chopped)
1/2 tsp. garlic powder
1/4 tsp. Kosher salt
1/4 tsp. freshly ground black pepper
2 Tbsp. olive oil
1 medium onion, chopped
3 cloves garlic (minced)
2 cups pasta sauce
2 Tbsp. capers (drained)
1/2 tsp. paprika (ground)
salt and freshly ground black pepper
fresh basil leaves

Method

1. In a stockpot over medium-high heat, cook spaghetti noodles in lightly salted boiling water, as directed in the package directions. Drain and set aside.
2. Combine the ground turkey breast, breadcrumbs, egg, parsley, garlic powder, salt, and pepper in a large bowl. Mix thoroughly. Shape turkey mixture into small balls. Set aside.
3. Heat oil in a large pot or saucepan over medium-high flame. Add the onion and garlic, stir-fry for until aromatic, about 3 minutes.
4. Add the turkey meatballs and cook until browned.
5. Add the pasta sauce, capers, and paprika. Cover with lid and then simmer for about 15-20 minutes, stirring occasionally. Season per to taste.
6. Divide spaghetti among serving plates. Top with meatball sauce. Garnish with fresh basil.
7. Serve and enjoy.

Nutritional Information:
Energy - 468 calories
Fat - 11.2 g
Carbohydrates - 65.4 g
Protein - 25.6 g
Sodium - 689 mg

Salmon Pasta and Broccoli Salad

Preparation Time: 10 minutes
Total Time: 30 minutes
Yield: 6 servings

Ingredients

4 cups penne pasta (cooked)
2 cups broccoli florets (steamed)
1 cup feta (diced)
8 oz. baked salmon (diced)
1 tsp. red peppercorns
salt and freshly ground black pepper

Lemon Vinaigrette Dressing:
1/3 cup olive oil
1/4 cup lemon juice
1 Tbsp. honey
1 tsp. fresh dill weed (chopped)

Method

1. Combine the pasta, broccoli, feta, salmon, and peppercorns in a large bowl. Season with salt and pepper to taste. Set aside.
2. In a small bowl, add all dressing ingredients and mix well. Pour this mixture into the salad. Toss to coat.
3. Divide among individual bowls.
4. Serve and enjoy.

Nutritional Information:
Energy - 356 calories
Fat - 19.3 g
Carbohydrates - 29.0 g
Protein - 16.6 g
Sodium - 319 mg

Baked Cod Fillet with Stewed Pumpkin

Preparation Time: 20 minutes
Total Time: 55 minutes
Yield: 4 servings

Ingredients

2 Tbsp. olive oil
2 Tbsp. lime juice
1 tsp. garlic powder
1/2 tsp. sage (dried)
4 (5 oz.) cod fillets
2 Tbsp. butter
1 large onion (thinly sliced)
2 cloves garlic (minced)
1 lb. sugar pumpkin (cut into small cubes)
2 cups organic chicken stock (low sodium)
1/2 tsp. paprika
1/2 tsp. cumin (ground)
salt and freshly ground black pepper
chopped fresh parsley

Method

1. Preheat your oven to 375 F.
2. Whisk together olive oil, lime juice, garlic powder, and sage in a small bowl. Set aside.
3. Place fish fillets in a baking dish, pat dry with paper towels. Pour olive oil mixture and brush to coat all sides. Season with of salt and pepper to taste. Bake in

the oven for about 15-20 minutes or until tested done (fish should be opaque and easily flaked using a fork).
4. Meanwhile, melt butter in a large pan or skillet over medium flame. Stir-fry onion and garlic for 3-5 minutes.
5. Add the pumpkin, chicken stock, paprika and cumin. Bring to a boil. Lower heat and simmer for 20-25 minutes. Season with salt and pepper. Remove from heat.
6. Serve cod fillets in individual plates with stewed pumpkin on the side. Sprinkle with fresh parsley.
7. Enjoy.

Nutritional Information:
Energy - 296 calories
Fat - 14.5 g
Carbohydrates - 14.9 g
Protein - 28.1 g
Sodium - 319 mg

Chicken and Pumpkin Stew

Preparation Time: 15 minutes
Total Time: 50 minutes
Yield: 6 servings

Ingredients

2 Tbsp. olive oil
1 large onion (chopped)
2 medium tomatoes (chopped)
3 cloves garlic (minced)
1 lb. chicken breast fillet (cut into strips)
1 lb. butternut pumpkin (cut into small cubes)
2 cups organic chicken stock (low sodium)
1 cup water
1 Tbsp. fresh thyme (chopped)
1 Tbsp. fresh rosemary (chopped)
salt and freshly ground black pepper

Method

1. Stir-fry onion for 3 minutes in a large saucepan over medium heat. Add tomatoes and garlic. Cook further 3 minutes, stirring often.
2. Add the chicken and stir-fry for 5-7 minutes.
3. Add the butternut pumpkin, chicken stock, water. Bring to a boil. Lower heat, cover with lid, and simmer for 25 minutes.
4. Add the herbs and cook further 5 minutes. Season with salt and pepper to taste. Remove from heat.
5. Ladle in individual bowls.

6. Serve and enjoy.

Nutritional Information:
Energy - 213 calories
Fat - 7.4 g
Carbohydrates - 14.1 g
Protein - 23.5 g
Sodium - 310 mg

Pumpkin Zucchini and Chickpea Stew with Feta

Preparation Time: 15 minutes
Total Time: 50 minutes
Yield: 6 servings

Ingredients

2 Tbsp. olive oil
2 shallots (chopped)
3 cloves garlic (minced)
1/2 sugar pumpkin (cut into small cubes)
2 medium zucchinis (thinly sliced)
2 cups canned chickpeas (drained)
2 cups organic beef stock (reduced-sodium)
2 cups water
1/2 tsp. coriander seed (ground)
1 cup feta cheese (diced)
salt and freshly ground black pepper

Method

1. Heat oil in a large in a large pot or saucepan over medium-high flame. Add the shallots and garlic; then stir-fry for 3-4 minutes.
2. Add the pumpkin, zucchinis, chickpeas, beef stock, water, and coriander seed. Bring to a boil. Lower heat and simmer for 25 minutes. Season with salt and pepper to taste. Remove from heat.
3. Ladle in individual bowls. Top with feta cheese.

4. Serve and enjoy.

Nutritional Information:
Energy - 238 calories
Fat - 11.9 g
Carbohydrates - 25.1 g
Protein - 10.7 g
Sodium - 359 mg

Spicy Beef and Pumpkin Stew

Preparation Time: 20 minutes
Total Time: 2 hours 20 minutes
Yield: 8 servings

Ingredients

2 Tbsp. olive oil
1 large red onion (sliced)
3 cloves garlic (minced)
2 lbs. beef sirloin (cubed)
2 stalks celery (diced)
3 cups organic beef stock (low sodium)
3 cups water
2 Tbsp. Worcestershire sauce
1 tsp. caraway seed
1 bay leaf
1 lb. sugar pumpkin (cut into small cubes)
1 medium red bell pepper
1 tsp. cayenne pepper
1/2 tsp. cumin (ground)
salt and freshly ground black pepper

Method

1. Heat oil in a large in a large saucepan over medium flame. Add the onion and garlic; then stir-fry for 3 minutes.

2. Add the beef and cook until browned about 7 minutes. Stir in stock, water, Worcestershire sauce, caraway, and bay leaf. Bring to a boil. Lower heat, cover with lid, and cook for 1 1/2 hours.
3. Add the pumpkin, bell pepper, cayenne, and cumin; cook for another 25-30 minutes. Season with salt and pepper to taste. Remove from heat.
4. Ladle in individual bowls.
5. Serve and enjoy.

Nutritional Information:
Energy - 287 calories
Fat - 11.1 g
Carbohydrates - 9.1 g
Protein - 36.6 g
Sodium - 320 mg

Tex-Mex Turkey Soup

Preparation Time: 10 minutes
Total Time: 50 minutes
Yield: 8 Servings

Ingredients:

For the Soup:

1 Tbsp. olive oil
1/2 medium sized onion - peeled and finely chopped
3 cloves garlic, minced
2 tsp. chili powder
1/2 tsp. cumin seeds
1/2 tsp. oregano
4 cups chicken stock
10.75 oz. can condensed tomato soup
28 ounce can diced tomatoes
1 cup salsa
2 cups turkey meat, cooked and shredded
1 Tbsp. dried parsley
2 cups frozen corn
3/4 cup canned white or black beans - drained and rinsed
1/2 cup light whipping cream
1/4 cup fresh cilantro, chopped

For Topping:

3 ounces corn tortilla chips
1 cup Cheddar-Monterey Jack cheese blend
1/2 cup sour cream

3/4 cup green onion, cut into rings
Some fresh parsley leaves
Some chopped scallions

Method:
1. Heat oil in the saucepan, add onions and sauté over medium heat until onions turn translucent and fragrant, about 2-4 minutes.
2. Stir in garlic, chili powder, cumin, oregano, and cook for about a minute more.
3. Add in stock, condensed tomato soup, diced tomatoes, salsa, shredded turkey, and parsley. Bring to a boil, and then mix in corns, black beans, sour cream and cilantro. Simmer for 20 to 30 minutes.
4. When soup is ready, pour it into serving bowls, top with tortilla chips, shredded cheese, and sour cream. Then arrange the onion rings in a decorative manner and sprinkle some fresh parsley leaves and chopped scallions. Serve warm.

Nutritional Information:
Energy - 347 calories
Fat - 12.1 g
Carbohydrates – 33.0 g
Protein – 28.3 g
Sodium - 564 mg

Pumpkin Soup with Cheddar

Preparation Time: 10 minutes
Total Time: 50 minutes
Yield: 8 servings

Ingredients

1 sugar pumpkin (peeled and cut into small cubes)
2 cups vegetable stock
2 cups half and half cream
1/2 tsp. onion powder
1/2 tsp. garlic powder
1/2 tsp. pumpkin pie spice
1/2 tsp. paprika
1/4 cup cilantro (chopped)
1/4 cup fresh parsley (minced)
1/4 cup butter (softened)
1/2 cup plain Greek yogurt
1/2 cup sour cream (for topping)
1/4 cup cheddar cheese (shredded)
salt and freshly ground black pepper
fresh parsley (for garnish)

Method

1. Combine the sugar pumpkin, vegetable stock, cream, onion powder, and garlic powder in a large saucepan. Bring to a boil. Reduce heat to a simmer. Cook for 25 minutes.

2. Stir in the pumpkin pie spice, paprika, cilantro, and parsley.
3. Gradually, add the butter, Greek yogurt and sour cream into the pumpkin mixture, stirring constantly. Remove from heat. Cool slightly. Transfer to your blender and process until smooth. (Blend in batches, if needed)
4. Return soup into the saucepan, stir in the cheddar cheese, and season with salt and pepper to taste. Cook for 3 minutes more.
5. Ladle in individual serving bowls.
6. Garnish with fresh parsley.
7. Serve and enjoy.

Nutritional Information:
Energy - 229 calories
Fat - 17.7 g
Carbohydrates - 13.7 g
Protein - 6.2 g
Sodium - 298 mg

Cheesy Broccoli and Cherry Tomato Quiche

Preparation Time: 10 minutes
Total Time: 50 minutes
Yield: 8 servings

Ingredients

1 baked pie shell
2 Tbsp. butter
2 shallots (finely chopped)
2 cloves garlic (crushed)
2 cups chopped broccoli florets
1 cup cherry tomatoes (halved)
1 cup cheddar cheese (grated)
6 large eggs
3 egg whites
1/2 cup of whole milk
salt and freshly ground black pepper

Method

1. Preheat your oven to 375 F.
2. Melt the butter in a large non-stick pan over medium heat. Add the shallots and garlic; then stir-fry until fragrant.
3. Add the broccoli and cherry tomatoes. Cook for 7-8 minutes while stirring occasionally. Transfer the vegetables into the pie shell and sprinkle with cheddar cheese on top.

4. Whisk together the eggs and whole milk. Season with salt and pepper to taste. Pour the mixture on top of cheese.
5. Bake for about 30 minutes or until set in the middle. Cool slightly before slicing.
6. Serve and enjoy.

Nutritional Information:
Energy – 242 calories
Fat - 16.8 g
Carbohydrates - 12.8 g
Protein - 12.3 g
Sodium - 345 mg

Chicken Mushroom and Leek Quiche

Preparation Time: 10 minutes
Total Time: 50 minutes
Yield: 8 servings

Ingredients

1 baked pie shell
2 Tbsp. olive oil
2 leeks (thinly sliced)
1 cup roasted chicken breast (shredded)
1 cup button mushroom (sliced)
1/4 cup fresh basil (coarsely chopped)
6 large eggs
3 egg whites
1/2 cup of half and half cream
1/4 cup parmesan cheese (finely grated)
1/2 cup cheddar cheese (grated)
salt and freshly ground black pepper

Method

1. Preheat your oven to 375 F.
2. Heat 2 tablespoons olive oil in a skillet or pan over medium flame. Stir-fry the leeks for 3-5 minutes.
3. Add the roasted chicken breast and mushrooms; cook, stirring often for 5 minutes. Season with salt and pepper to taste. Remove from heat. Transfer into the pie shell.
4. Beat the eggs and stir in half and half cream and parmesan cheese. Season with salt and pepper to

taste. Gently pour the egg mixture on top of chicken-leek mixture. Sprinkle with cheddar cheese.
5. Cook in the oven for about 30 minutes or until set in the middle. Cool slightly before slicing.
6. Serve and enjoy.

Nutritional Information:

Energy - 298 calories

Fat - 18.1 g

Carbohydrates - 12.7 g

Protein - 22.1 g

Sodium - 327 mg

Chunky Chicken and Apple Salad

Preparation Time: 10 minutes
Total Time: 40 minutes
Yield: 6 servings

Ingredients

1 ½ lb. chicken meat, cooked and diced
1 small red apple, cored and diced
1 small green apple, cored and diced
4 celery stalks, chopped
A handful of crushed walnuts
1 tsp. garlic powder
1 Tbsp. fresh parsley, chopped
1 tsp. cayenne pepper
salt and freshly ground pepper

Dressing:
2 egg yolks
2 Tbsp. Dijon mustard
2 Tbsp. lemon juice
1 Tbsp. chipotle sauce
1/3 cup olive oil
salt and freshly ground pepper

Method

1. Prepare the dressing: combine the egg yolks, Dijon mustard, lemon juice, and chipotle sauce. Season with salt and pepper. Using a hand mixer, gradually

whisk in the olive oil until you have a mayonnaise consistency.
2. Place the chicken in a large bowl. Add the apples, celery, walnuts, garlic powder, parsley, and cayenne pepper. Season to taste.
3. Add the prepared dressing and toss to combine.
4. Chill for at least 1-2 hours before serving.

Nutritional Information:
Energy - 320 calories
Fat - 17.2 g
Carbohydrates - 12.7 g
Protein - 32.8 g
Sodium - 257 mg

Zucchini Tomato and Feta Salad

Preparation Time: 15 minutes
Total Time: 15 minutes
Yield: 4 servings

Ingredients

2 baby zucchinis (shaved)
2 cups grape tomatoes (halved)
1 small head iceberg lettuce (torn)
1 cup crumbled feta

Dressing:
1/4 cup olive oil
2 Tbsp. red wine vinegar
1 Tbsp. lemon juice
2 tsp. honey

Method

1. Place the zucchinis, grape tomatoes, lettuce, and feta in a large bowl. Toss to combine well.
2. In a small bowl. Whisk together all dressing ingredients.
3. Divide salad among 4 individual plates. Drizzle with prepared dressing.
4. Serve immediately and enjoy.

Nutritional Information:
Energy - 233 calories

Fat - 14.7 g
Carbohydrates - 13.6 g
Protein - 13.8 g
Sodium - 361 mg

Rocket Peach and Feta Salad

Preparation Time: 15 minutes
Total Time: 15 minutes
Yield: 4 servings

Ingredients

4 cups baby rocket (leaves separated)
4 peach halves (diced)
1 medium red bell pepper (thinly sliced)
1/2 fennel bulb (shaved)
1 cup herbed feta cheese (diced)

Dressing:
1/4 cup olive oil
2 Tbsp. lemon juice
1 Tbsp. Dijon mustard
2 tsp. honey

Method

1. Place the rocket, peaches, bell pepper, fennel, and feta cheese in a large bowl. Toss to combine well.
2. Whisk the olive oil, along with the 2 tablespoons lemon juice, 1 tablespoon Dijon mustard, and 2 teaspoons honey in a small bowl.
3. Divide salad among 4 individual plates. Drizzle with prepared dressing.
4. Serve immediately and enjoy.

Nutritional Information:
Energy - 306 calories
Fat - 21.3 g
Carbohydrates - 25.0 g
Protein - 7.8 g
Sodium - 390 mg

Fresh Italian Garden Salad

Preparation Time: 15 minutes
Total Time: 15 minutes
Yield: 4 servings

Ingredients

2 cups fresh sweet basil (leaves separated)
3 cups cherry tomatoes (halved)
1 medium red bell pepper (thinly sliced)
1/2 cup black olives (sliced)
1 cup crumbled feta cheese

Dressing:
1/4 cup olive oil
2 Tbsp. balsamic vinegar
1 tsp. Dijon mustard
1 tsp. honey
1/4 tsp. Italian seasoning

Method

1. Place the fresh basil, cherry tomatoes, bell pepper, olives, and crumbled feta cheese in a large bowl. Toss to combine well.
2. Whisk together the olive oil, 2 Tbsp. balsamic vinegar, Dijon mustard, honey, and Italian seasoning in a small bowl.
3. Divide salad among 3 individual plates. Drizzle with prepared dressing.

4. Serve immediately and enjoy.

Nutritional Information:
Energy - 272 calories
Fat - 22.9 g
Carbohydrates - 12.0 g
Protein - 7.4 g
Sodium - 588 mg

Red Cabbage Slaw with Pomegranates

Preparation Time: 10 minutes
Total Time: 15 minutes
Yield: 4 servings

Ingredients

For the dressing:

1/4 cup apple cider vinegar

1/4 cup raw honey

3 Tbsp. olive oil

2 Tbsp. balsamic vinegar

1 garlic clove, minced

1 tsp. Dijon mustard

1/2 tsp. salt

1/4 tsp. black pepper

For the slaw:

1 small head red cabbage, shredded

1 carrot, peeled and grated

1 cup pomegranate seeds

1/4 cup sunflower seeds

Method

1. In a sauce pan combine all the dressing ingredients. Bring to a simmer over medium flame and cook for 3 minutes. Turn off the heat and let the dressing to cool.
2. Prepare the slaw: shred the cabbage and the carrot. Place them in a large bowl.

3. Add the pomegranate seeds and sunflower seeds. Pour the dressing over. Toss to coat.
4. Serve and enjoy.

Nutritional Information:

Energy - 272 calories

Fat - 22.9 g

Carbohydrates - 12.0 g

Protein - 7.4 g

Sodium - 588 mg

Chicken Macaroni Salad with Mixed Veggies

Preparation Time: 20 minutes
Total Time: 2 hours 20 minutes
Yield: 6 servings

Ingredients

4 cups cooked macaroni noodles
1 cup chicken ham (chopped)
1 cup frozen vegetable mix (blanched and drained)
3/4 cup light mayonnaise
6 oz. plain Greek yogurt
1 shallot (minced)
1/2 cup cheddar cheese (grated)
1/2 cup crushed pineapple (drained)
2 Tbsp. sweet pickle relish
salt and freshly ground black pepper

Method

1. In a large bowl, place the macaroni, chicken ham, vegetable mix, mayonnaise, cheese, pineapple, pickle relish, and shallot. Toss to combine well. Season with salt and pepper to taste. Cover with plastic wrap. Chill for at least 2-3 hours or until it is ready to serve.
2. Transfer to a serving dish.
3. Serve and enjoy.

Nutritional Information:
Energy - 297 calories

Fat - 16.4 g
Carbohydrates - 26.7 g
Protein - 11.5 g
Sodium - 523 mg

Zucchini Muffins with Turkey Ham

Preparation Time: 10 minutes
Total Time: 35 minutes
Yield: 6 servings

Ingredients

1 ½ cups all-purpose flour

2 tsp. baking powder

1 tsp. baking soda

1/2 tsp. salt

2 whole eggs

1/4 cup water

1/2 cup olive oil

1 zucchini, trimmed and grated

2 oz. chopped turkey ham

2 Tbsp. chopped sun-dried tomatoes

Method

1. Preheat oven to 350 F and line 6-hole muffin tin with paper cases.
2. In a bowl, combine the flour, baking powder, baking soda, and salt.
3. In a separate bowl whisk the eggs along with the water and oil. Then, pour the liquid ingredients into a dry ones and stir until combined well.
4. Fold in the zucchini, ham and sun-dried tomatoes. Stir well.

5. Spoon the mixture into prepared muffin tin and bake in preheated oven for 25 minutes.
6. Transfer the muffin tin to a wire rack and cool for 10 minutes.
7. Remove the muffins from the tin and serve at room temperature.

Nutritional Information:
Energy - 272 calories
Fat - 22.9 g
Carbohydrates - 12.0 g
Protein - 7.4 g
Sodium - 588 mg

Cheesy Mini Mediterranean Pizza

Preparation time: 15 minutes
Total time: 15 minutes
Yield: 16 servings

Ingredients

16 thin slices of French bread
3/4 cup pizza sauce
16 thin slices of red bell pepper
1 cup button mushrooms, thinly sliced
1/2 cup olives, drained and thinly sliced
1/2 cup mozzarella cheese, grated
1/2 cup cheddar cheese, grated
16 basil leaves

Method

1. Spread pizza sauce onto one side of each bread slice.
2. Top with red bell pepper, mushrooms, and olives.
3. Sprinkle with mozzarella and cheddar cheese.
4. Bake in the oven for 8 minutes or until the cheese has melted. Garnish with fresh basil.
5. Place in a serving platter.
6. Serve and enjoy.

Nutritional Information:

Energy - 272 calories
Fat - 22.9 g

Carbohydrates - 12.0 g
Protein - 7.4 g
Sodium - 588 mg

Vegetable and Cheddar Kebabs

Preparation time: 15 minutes
Total time: 15 minutes
Yield: 16 servings

Ingredients

16 cherry tomatoes

16 thin slices (round) cucumber

16 black olives

8 oz. cheddar cheese, cubed

Method

1. Thread 1 of each - olive, cucumber, cheese, and cherry tomato on each toothpick or skewer.
2. Place in a serving dish.
3. Serve and enjoy.

Nutritional Information:

Energy - 272 calories

Fat - 22.9 g

Carbohydrates - 12.0 g

Protein - 7.4 g

Sodium - 588 mg

Homemade Gingerbread Cookies

Preparation Time: 10 minutes
Total Time: 1 hour 30 minutes
Yield: 40 servings

Ingredients

1 cup butter (softened)
1 1/2 cups white sugar
2 Tbsp. light corn syrup
1 medium egg
3 cups all-purpose flour
2 tsp. baking soda
1 1/2 tsp. ginger (ground)
1 1/2 tsp. cinnamon (ground)
1 tsp. cloves (ground)
1/4 tsp. allspice (ground)
2 egg whites
1/2 tsp. cream of tartar
2 cups powdered sugar
cooking oil spray

Method

1. In a large bowl, place the butter, sugar and corn syrup. Beat using an electric mixer until you get a creamy and smooth texture. Add the egg and whisk thorough until well blended.
2. In another bowl, combine the flour, baking soda, ginger, cinnamon, cloves and allspice. Gradually, stir

into the creamed mixture. Cover with plastic wrap and keep refrigerated for at least 1/2 hour.
3. Preheat your oven to 375 F. Grease cookie sheets with oil spray.
4. Roll the dough out to 1/4 inch in thickness on a floured surface then cut into desired shapes with cookie cutters.
5. Place cookies 1 ½ to 2 inches apart onto the cookie sheets.
6. Bake for 8 minutes in the oven. Let the cookies cool on baking sheet for about 5 to 7 minutes before transferring them to a wire rack to cool completely.
7. To make the frosting, beat egg whites and cream of tartar until foamy.
8. Slowly add the sugar and continue beating until icing becomes stiff enough to hold. You may add food coloring if desired. Pipe icing onto each cooled cookies. It can also be used to attach candy decorations.
9. Serve and enjoy.

Nutritional Information:
Energy - 132 calories
Fat - 4.8 g
Carbohydrates - 21.6 g
Protein - 1.3 g
Sodium - 99 mg

Easy Sugar Cookies

Preparation Time: 10 minutes
Total Time: 40 minutes
Yield: 24 servings

Ingredients

1 1/4 cups white sugar

1 cup butter

3 medium egg yolks

1 tsp. vanilla or almond extract

2 1/2 cups all-purpose flour

1 tsp. baking soda

1/2 tsp. cream of tartar

cooking oil spray

Method

1. Preheat your oven to 350 F. Lightly grease 2 cookie sheets with oil spray.
2. Cream together sugar and butter using an electric mixer.
3. Whisk in egg yolks and vanilla extract until blended well.
4. Slowly add the flour, baking soda, and cream of tartar.
5. Shape dough into walnut size balls and arrange them at least 2 inches apart on the cookie sheet. No need to flatten.
6. Bake in the oven for 10 to 11 minutes, or until tops are cracked and just turning golden brown. Remove from

heat. Set aside for 10 minutes then cool completely in wire racks.
7. Serve and enjoy or store in airtight container.

Nutritional Information:
Energy - 162 calories
Fat - 8.4 g
Carbohydrates - 20.5 g
Protein - 1.8 g
Sodium - 108 mg

Holiday Chocolate Chip Cookies

Preparation Time: 15 minutes
Total Time: 1 hour 40 minutes
Yield: 72 servings

Ingredients

4 1/2 cups all-purpose flour

2 tsp. baking soda

2 cups butter (softened)

1 1/2 cups brown sugar (packed)

1/2 cup granulated sugar

2 (3.4 oz.) packages of vanilla pudding instant mix

4 whole eggs

2 tsp. pure vanilla extract

4 cups semisweet chocolate chips

Method

1. Preheat your oven to 350 F.
2. Sift the flour and baking soda together in a mixing bowl. Set aside.
3. Place the 2 cups butter, 1 ½ cups brown sugar, and ½ cup granulated sugar in a large bowl. Beat mixture with an electric mixer until you get a smooth texture.
4. Add the instant pudding mix and whip until blended.
5. Stir in the eggs and vanilla extract. Slowly, add the flour mixture.
6. Fold in the chocolate chips. With a small ice cream scoop, drop cookies onto ungreased cookie sheets.

7. Place in the preheated oven and cook for 10 to 12 minutes. Remove from heat. Set aside for 10 minutes then cool completely in wire racks.
8. Serve and enjoy or store in airtight container.

Nutritional Information:
Energy - 158 calories
Fat - 9.0 g
Carbohydrates - 18.5 g
Protein - 1.3 g
Sodium - 78 mg

Peanut Butter Christmas Cookies

Preparation Time: 15 minutes
Total Time: 1 hour 25 minutes
Yield: 48 servings

Ingredients

1 cup unsalted butter
1 1/2 cup peanut butter
1 cup white sugar
1 cup packed brown sugar
2 whole eggs
1 tsp. pure vanilla extract
3 cups all-purpose flour
1 tsp. baking powder
1/2 tsp. Kosher salt
1 1/2 tsp. baking soda

Method

1. Preheat your oven to 375 F.
2. Mix together butter, peanut butter, and sugars in a large bowl, using an electric mixer, until creamy. Add the eggs one by one, then stir in the vanilla extract.
3. Next sift the all-purpose flour, baking powder, baking soda, and salt in a medium bowl. Add into butter mixture. Mix well. Cover the cookie dough and refrigerate for about an hour.
4. On a floured work surface, roll dough into 1/4-inch thick. Using a cookie cutter, cut dough to desired

Christmas shapes. Arrange in baking sheets leaving 2 inches apart.
5. Bake in the oven for about 10 minutes or until cookies starts to brown.
6. Remove from heat. Let sit for 10 minutes then cool completely in wire racks.
7. Serve and enjoy or store in airtight container.

Nutritional Information:
Energy - 140 calories
Fat - 8.2 g
Carbohydrates - 14.8 g
Protein - 3.1 g
Sodium - 129 mg

Holiday Molasses Cookies

Preparation Time: 10 minutes
Total Time: 1 hour 20 minutes
Yield: 30 servings

Ingredients

3/4 cup butter (melted)
1 cup white sugar
1 whole egg
1/4 cup molasses
2 1/4 cups all-purpose flour
1 tsp. baking soda
1/2 tsp. Kosher salt
3/4 tsp. cinnamon (ground)
3/4 tsp. cloves (ground)
3/4 tsp. ginger (ground)
1/2 cup powdered sugar
cooking oil spray

Method

1. In a medium bowl, combine together the melted butter, 1 cup sugar, and egg until smooth. Add the molasses and mix well.
2. In a separate bowl, combine the all-purpose flour, baking soda, salt, and spices. Stir into the molasses mixture. Cover with plastic wrap, and chill dough for an hour.
3. Preheat oven to 375 F.

4. Roll dough to 1/4-inch thick, and then cut out to desired holiday shapes using a cookie cutter. Place cookies 2 inches apart from each other onto ungreased baking sheets.
5. Bake for about 8 to 10 minutes in the oven. Let sit for a few minutes before moving the cookies into wire racks to cool completely. Dust with some powdered sugar.
6. Serve and enjoy.

Nutritional Information:
Energy - 118 calories
Fat - 49 g
Carbohydrates - 18.0 g
Protein - 10.2 g
Sodium - 116 mg

Bread Pudding with Dried Cranberries

Preparation Time: 15 minutes
Total Time: 1 hour 55 minutes
Yield: 12 servings

Ingredients

3 1/2 cups milk

1 cup heavy cream

3/4 cup white sugar

5 whole eggs

1 1/2 tsp. lemon zest

1/2 tsp. salt

1/4 tsp. cinnamon (ground)

1 tsp. almond extract

1 1/2 French baguettes (cut into 2-inch pieces)

1 cup cranberries

1/2 cup seedless raisins

2 tsp. butter

Method

1. Whisk together the milk, heavy cream, 3/4 cup sugar, eggs, zest, salt, cinnamon, and almond extract in a bowl.
2. Stir in baguette, cranberries, and raisins. Let sit to soak for 45 minutes.
3. Preheat your oven to 350 F. Grease a 12-inch deep round casserole dish with butter.
4. Pour the bread mixture onto prepared dish then cover with aluminum foil.

5. Bake in the oven for 45 minutes. Remove foil and bake for another 10-15 minutes or until pudding is set and golden brown.

Nutritional Information:
Energy - 221 calories
Fat - 8.0 g
Carbohydrates - 31.6 g
Protein - 7.0 g
Sodium - 273 mg

Spiced Almond Pumpkin Waffles

Preparation Time: 15 minutes
Total Time: 20 minutes
Yield: 4 servings

Ingredients

1/4 cup coconut milk
2 eggs (whisked)
2 Tbsp. raw honey
1 Tbsp. pure vanilla paste
1/2 cup pureed pumpkin
3/4 cup almond flour
1/4 cup shredded unsweetened coconut
1/2 tsp. ground cinnamon
1/4 tsp. ground ginger
1/4 tsp. baking soda

Method

1. Preheat the waffle iron.
2. In a bowl whisk the coconut milk, eggs, honey, vanilla paste and pumpkin puree.
3. In a separate bowl whisk the almond flour, shredded coconut, cinnamon, ginger and baking soda. Fold the dry ingredients into a pumpkin mixture and give it all a good stir until blended.
4. Pour around ¼ cup batter into waffle iron and cook for 3-4 minutes.
5. Serve while still hot.

Nutritional Information:
Energy - 298 calories
Fat - 18.1 g
Carbohydrates - 12.7 g
Protein - 22.1 g
Sodium - 327 mg

Carrot Walnut Cupcake with Cinnamon

Preparation Time: 30 minutes
Total Time: 1 hour 55 minutes
Yield: 24 servings

Ingredients
2 whole eggs (lightly beaten)
1 cup granulated sugar
1/3 cup brown sugar
1/2 cup vegetable oil
1 tsp. pure vanilla extract
2 cups carrots (shredded)
1/2 cup crushed pineapple (drained)
1 1/2 cups all-purpose flour
2 tsp. baking powder
1 1/4 tsp. baking soda
1/2 tsp. Kosher salt
1 1/2 tsp. cinnamon (ground)
1/2 tsp. nutmeg (ground)
1/4 tsp. ginger (ground)
2/3 cup walnuts (chopped)
cooking oil spray

Cream Cheese Icing:
2 oz. white chocolate
1 (8 oz.) package cream cheese, softened
1/2 cup unsalted butter (softened)
1 tsp. orange extract

2 cups powdered sugar

1 Tbsp. heavy cream

Method
1. Preheat oven to 350 F. Lightly grease two 12 muffin cups with oil spray.
2. Melt white chocolate over low heat, in a small saucepan. Stir until you get a smooth texture, and then cool at room temperature.
3. Meanwhile, combine the cream cheese and butter in a large bowl. Beat until smooth. Next stir in white chocolate and orange extract.
4. Gradually add the powdered sugar and beat until it becomes fluffy; then add the heavy cream. Cover and keep in the chiller until ready to use.
5. In a large bowl, beat together the eggs, granulated sugar, and brown sugar. Mix in the oil and vanilla. Stir in carrots and crushed pineapple.
6. In a separate bowl, combine together the flour, baking powder, baking soda, Kosher salt, cinnamon, nutmeg, and ginger. Gently add the flour mixture into the carrot mixture until incorporated well, then fold in 1/2 cup walnuts. Spoon cupcake batter onto the prepared muffin cups, about 2/3 full.
7. Bake for 25 minutes in the oven, or until tested done. Cool completely on wire racks before topping with prepared icing.
8. Serve and enjoy.

Nutritional Information:
Energy - 262 calories
Fat - 15.2 g
Carbohydrates - 29.8 g
Protein - 3.1 g
Sodium - 186 mg

Honey Cake with Walnuts

Preparation Time: 25 minutes
Total Time: 1 hour 10 minutes
Yield: 20 servings

Ingredients

2 1/2 cups all-purpose flour

1 Tbsp. baking powder

1/2 tsp. baking soda

1/2 tsp. salt

1 tsp. cinnamon (ground)

1 cup honey

1 cup brown sugar

1/2 cup vegetable oil

4 whole eggs

1 cup fresh orange juice

2 tsp. orange zest (finely grated)

3/4 cup walnuts (coarsely chopped)

Method

1. Preheat oven to 350 F. Grease and flour two loaf pans.
2. In a medium bowl, sift the flour, baking powder, baking soda, salt and cinnamon together. Set aside.
3. Whisk brown sugar, honey, oil, eggs and orange zest together in a large bowl. Stir in the flour mixture alternately with the orange juice, mixing just until combined.
4. Fold in walnuts. Pour batter mixture into prepared pan.

5. Bake in the oven for 40 to 50 minutes, or until tested done. Let cool in wire rack before slicing.
6. Serve and enjoy.

Nutritional Information:
Energy - 242 calories
Fat - 9.3 g
Carbohydrates - 38.2 g
Protein - 4.0 g
Sodium - 105 mg

Pumpkin Muffin with Whipped Cream Topping

Preparation Time: 25 minutes
Total Time: 55 minutes
Yield: 24 servings

Ingredients

3 1/2 cups all-purpose flour

2 tsp. baking soda

1 tsp. baking powder

1 tsp. Kosher salt

1 1/2 tsp. cinnamon (ground)

1 tsp. allspice (ground)

1 tsp. nutmeg (ground)

1/2 tsp. cloves (ground)

2 cups canned pumpkin puree

1 1/2 cups white sugar

1/2 cup light brown sugar

1/2 cup applesauce

1 cup Greek yogurt (vanilla)

4 egg whites

1 whole egg

2/3 cup water

1 cup seedless raisins

1 cup whipped cream or icing (for topping)

1/4 cup candy sprinkles (for topping)

Method

1. Preheat your oven to 350 F. Line two 12-cup muffin tins with baking paper.

2. In a medium bowl, combine together the flour, baking soda, baking powder, Kosher salt, cinnamon, allspice, nutmeg, and cloves.
3. In a large bowl, beat together the pumpkin, white sugar, brown sugar, applesauce, Greek yogurt, egg whites, and egg using an electric mixer.
4. Gradually add the flour mixture into the sugar mixture, alternating it with water.
5. Fold in raisins. Spoon batter mixture onto the prepared muffin tins.
6. Bake for about 16 to 18 minutes in the oven, until tested done. Transfer in wire racks to cool.
7. Top with whipped cream and candy sprinkles.
8. Serve and enjoy.

Nutritional Information:
Energy - 185 calories
Fat - 2.5 g
Carbohydrates - 38.0 g
Protein - 4.2 g
Sodium - 217 mg

Cinnamon Rolls with Dried Cherries and Almonds

Preparation Time: 20 minutes
Total Time: 1 hour 30 minutes
Yield: 24 servings

Ingredients

3/4 cup whole milk

1/4 cup butter (softened)

3 1/4 cups all-purpose flour

1 (.25 oz.) package instant yeast

1/2 cup white sugar

1/2 tsp. Kosher salt

1/4 cup water

1 whole egg

1 cup brown sugar (packed)

1 Tbsp. cinnamon (ground)

1/2 cup butter (softened)

1/2 cup dried cherries

1/2 cup almonds (chopped)

Method

1. Heat the milk in a small saucepan to a simmer, then remove from heat. Stir in butter until melted. Let cool to lukewarm.
2. In a large mixing bowl, combine together the 2 1/4 cup flour, yeast, white sugar, and Kosher salt. Mix well.

3. Add water, egg, and the milk mixture. Mix well. Add the remaining flour, about 1/2 cup at a time, mixing well every after each addition. When the dough has just come together, transfer it into a lightly floured surface and knead dough until smooth, about 5 to 7 minutes.
4. Cover dough with a damp kitchen towel and let sit for 10 minutes.
5. Meanwhile, mix together brown sugar, cinnamon, and softened butter in a small bowl,
6. Roll out dough to make a 12x9 inch rectangle. Spread butter-sugar mixture on top of dough. Sprinkle with dried cherries and almonds. Roll the dough and pinch the sides to seal. Cut evenly into 24 rolls and place cut side up in 12 lightly greased muffin cups. Cover rolls and let them rise until they are doubled in size, about 30 minutes. Preheat your oven to 375 F.
7. Bake in the oven until golden brown, about 18-20 minutes. Remove from muffin cups to cool.
8. Serve warm and enjoy.

Nutritional Information:
Energy - 192 calories
Fat - 7.4 g
Carbohydrates - 27.4 g
Protein - 2.9 g
Sodium - 99 mg

Traditional Pecan Pie with Maple Syrup

Preparation Time: 25 minutes
Total Time: 1 hour
Yield: 12 servings

Ingredients

1 1/2 cups all-purpose flour

1/2 tsp. salt

2 Tbsp. white sugar

1/2 cup butter (chilled)

4 Tbsp. ice water

3 whole eggs (beaten)

3/4 cup maple syrup

3/4 cup brown sugar (packed)

3 Tbsp. butter (melted)

1 tsp. pure vanilla extract

1/4 tsp. salt

1/2 cup finely chopped pecans

1 cup pecans (quartered)

1 cup pecan halves

Method

1. Preheat your oven to 350 F.
2. Prepare the crust by combining flour, salt and white sugar in a large bowl. Add butter and cut into the flour mixture until it resembles coarse crumbs. Gradually, sprinkle with water, stirring until dough comes together just enough to form a ball.

3. On a floured work surface, flatten dough using a rolling pin. Roll out to make a circle about an inch larger than your pie dish. Place the pie shell into dish and keep refrigerated until pie filling is complete.
4. Prepare the pecan pie filling by mixing together the eggs, maple syrup, brown sugar, butter, vanilla extract, salt, and finely chopped pecans. Add the quartered pecans and spread at the bottom of refrigerated pie crust. Pour the egg-syrup mixture over pecans, then top with pecan halves.
5. Bake in the oven for one hour or until firm. Allow to cool before serving.
6. Enjoy.

Nutritional Information:
Energy - 318 calories
Fat - 17.8 g
Carbohydrates - 37.4 g
Protein - 4.0 g
Sodium - 242 mg

Homemade Scones with Chocolate Chips and Walnuts

Preparation Time: 15 minutes
Total Time: 35 minutes
Yield: 12 servings

Ingredients

1 1/2 cups all-purpose flour

1/3 cup light brown sugar

1 1/2 tsp. baking powder

3/4 tsp. bicarbonate of soda

1/4 tsp. Kosher salt

1/3 cup butter (unsalted)

1/2 cup buttermilk

1 whole egg

1 1/2 tsp. vanilla extract

1 cup semisweet chocolate chips

1/2 cup walnuts (chopped)

Method

1. Preheat your oven to 400 F. Grease a 10-inch circle in the middle of a baking sheet with butter.
2. Mix the flour, brown sugar, baking powder, bicarbonate of soda, and salt in a large mixing bowl
3. Cut the butter into small pieces, and place on top of flour the mixture. With a pastry cutter, mix together the flour mixture and butter.

4. Add the buttermilk, egg, and vanilla extract. Mix well. Stir in the chocolate chips and walnuts. The resulting dough should be sticky.
5. Place the dough into the 10-inch diameter circle on the baking sheet. Cut with a serrated knife to make 12 equal wedges.
6. Bake in the oven for about 18 to 20 minutes, or until it is golden brown. Cool slightly.
7. Serve warm and enjoy.

Nutritional Information:
Energy - 254 calories
Fat - 14.1 g
Carbohydrates - 29.3 g
Protein - 3.7 g
Sodium - 184 mg

Fresh Peach Pie Home-Style

Preparation Time: 20 minutes
Total Time: 45 minutes
Yield: 12 servings

Ingredients

2 pie pastry dough (for 9-inch pie crust)

1 1/4 cup white sugar

1 cup water

1/4 cup cornstarch

1 1/2 Tbsp. butter

2 cups fresh peaches (pitted and mashed)

1 tsp. pure vanilla extract

1/4 tsp. cinnamon (ground)

1/4 tsp. nutmeg (ground)

4 cups peaches (peeled, pitted, and sliced thinly)

Method

1. Preheat your oven to 375 F.
2. Roll out 1 pie pastry dough and place into the bottom of a pie pan. Set aside.
3. Mix together the sugar, water, cornstarch, butter, mashed peaches, vanilla extract, cinnamon, and nutmeg in a saucepan. Bring to a boil. Lower heat and simmer until clear and thick, stirring often.
4. Fill the pie with sliced fresh peaches, alternating with the prepared peach glaze.
5. Roll out the remaining pastry dough and cover the filling sealing the edges with a fork.

6. Place in the preheated oven and bake for 15-20 minutes or until golden brown. Remove from heat and place into a wire rack to cool slightly before cutting.
7. Serve and enjoy.

Nutritional Information:
Energy - 246 calories
Fat - 9.0 g
Carbohydrates - 41.4 g
Protein - 1.7 g
Sodium - 155 mg

Rustic Apple Pie Home-Style

Preparation Time: 25 minutes
Total Time: 1 hour 10 minutes
Yield: 12 servings

Ingredients
1 1/2 cups all-purpose flour
1/2 cup canola oil
2 Tbsp. cold milk
1 1/2 tsp. white sugar
1 tsp. Kosher salt
6 green apples (cored and sliced)
3/4 cup brown sugar
3 Tbsp. all-purpose flour
3/4 tsp. cinnamon (ground)
1/2 tsp. nutmeg (ground)
1/2 cup all-purpose flour
1/2 cup white sugar
1/2 cup butter

Method
1. Preheat oven to 350 F.
2. *To Prepare the Crust:* In a large mixing bowl, mix together 1 1/2 cups flour, vegetable oil, milk, 1 1/2 teaspoons sugar, and salt until combined well. Spread the pie crust mixture evenly over the bottom and up to the sides of a 9-inch pie pan, pressing lightly and crimping edges.

3. ***To Make the Apple Pie Filling:*** Mix together 3/4 cup brown sugar, 3 tablespoons flour, cinnamon, and nutmeg in a separate bowl. Sprinkle the brown sugar mixture over apples and toss to coat. Place in unbaked pie shell and spread evenly.
4. ***To Make the Topping:*** Using a pastry cutter, combine together 1/2 cup flour, 1/2 cup sugar and butter until mixed well and becomes crumbly. Top mixture over apples.
5. Place the apple pie in the preheated oven with a cookie sheet at the bottom to catch the juices that may spill over. Bake for 45 minutes.
6. Allow the apple pie to cool before slicing.
7. Serve and enjoy.

Nutritional Information:
Energy - 332 calories
Fat - 14.2 g
Carbohydrates - 50.8 g
Protein - 2.8 g
Sodium - 253 mg

Luscious Cranberry Pie

Preparation Time: 20 minutes
Total Time: 1 hour 15 minutes
Yield: 12 servings

Ingredients

1 (10-inch) unbaked pie crust
1 (8 oz.) package cream cheese (softened)
1 cup all-purpose cream
1 (14 oz.) can sweetened condensed milk
1 whole egg
1/4 cup lemon juice
1/4 cup granulated sugar
2 Tbsp. cornstarch
1 (16-ounce) can of cranberry sauce (whole berry)
3/4 cup fresh cranberries

Method

1. Preheat oven to 400 F.
2. Bake unbaked pie crust in the preheated oven 8-10 minutes. Remove from heat. Reduce oven temperature to 375 F.
3. In a large bowl, beat cream cheese using an electric mixer until fluffy. Add the cream, sweetened condensed milk, egg and lemon juice. Mix well. Transfer mixture into the pie crust.
4. In a small bowl, mix together 1 tablespoon granulated sugar and cornstarch. Stir in whole berry cranberry

sauce. Spread the mixture evenly over cream cheese mixture. Top with fresh cranberries.
5. Bake for 45 minutes oven, or until bubbly and the crust is lightly browned. Cool the cranberry pie on a wire rack before slicing.
6. Serve enjoy.

Nutritional Information:
Energy - 294 calories
Fat - 13.9 g
Carbohydrates - 36.3 g
Protein - 5.2 g
Sodium - 177 mg

Orange Pumpkin Pie

Preparation Time: 10 minutes
Total Time: 1 hour 25 minutes
Yield: 10 servings

Ingredients

1 pie pastry crust (baked)
2 whole eggs and 1 egg yolk
1/4 cup fresh orange juice
3/4 cup of packed brown sugar
1/2 tsp. orange zest (finely grated)
1/2 tsp. of salt
1 tsp. cinnamon (ground)
1/2 tsp. ginger (ground)
1/4 tsp. cloves (ground)
1/4 tsp. cardamom (ground)
1/4 tsp. nutmeg (ground)
2 1/4 cups of pumpkin puree
1 1/4 cups of heavy cream

Method

1. Preheat your oven to 425°F.
2. Beat the eggs and yolk in a bowl and whisk in the orange juice and brown sugar.
3. Stir in the lemon zest, salt, and spices. Add the puree and the cream. Mix all ingredients well.
4. Pour the pumpkin filling into the pie crust and bake for 15 minutes. Lower the oven temperature to 350 F and bake for another 40-45 minutes. Allow to cool

before slicing. Top with a spoonful of sour cream or yogurt, if desired.
5. Serve and enjoy.

Nutritional Information:
Energy - 315 calories
Fat - 11.6 g
Carbohydrates - 42.8 g
Protein – 4.2 g
Sodium - 253 mg

Apple Pie Ala Mode

Preparation Time: 15 minutes
Total Time: 1 hour 10 minutes
Yield: 10 servings

Ingredients
2 pie pastry dough (for 9-inch pie crust)
6 green apples (cored and sliced)
3/4 cup brown sugar
3 Tbsp. all-purpose flour
1 tsp. cinnamon (ground)
1/2 tsp. nutmeg (ground)
1/4 cup egg wash
vanilla ice cream

Method
1. Preheat oven to 350 F.
2. Roll out and place 1 pie pastry dough in the bottom up to the sides of a 9-inch pie pan, pressing lightly and crimping edges. Set aside.
3. Combine the 3/4 cup brown sugar, all-purpose flour, cinnamon, and nutmeg together in a separate bowl. Add the apples and toss to coat. Transfer mixture into the unbaked pie shell, spreading evenly.
4. Roll the remaining pie pastry dough and place on top of filling to cover. Seal the edges using a fork. Make a few slits in the middle of the pie, and then brush the entire top with egg wash.

5. Bake the apple pie in the preheated oven for 40-45 minutes. Then cool for a few minutes before slicing.
6. Serve pie with a scoop of vanilla ice cream on top.
7. Enjoy.

Nutritional Information:
Energy - 273 calories
Fat - 9.9 g
Carbohydrates - 45.6 g
Protein - 2.5 g
Sodium - 183 mg

Turtle Pie Cheesecake with Pecans

Preparation Time: 20 minutes
Total Time: 5 hours 45 minutes
Yield: 12 servings

Ingredients

2 cups Oreo cookies (finely crushed)

1/3 cup butter (melted)

1/3 cup milk

1 cup soft caramel candies

2 (8 oz. each) cream cheese (softened)

1 cup cream

3/4 cup white sugar

2 tsp. vanilla

3 whole eggs

1 cup pecan halves

chocolate syrup, to serve

Method

1. Preheat your oven to 325 F.
2. Mix crumbs and butter in a medium bowl. Spread this mixture onto the bottom and press about 2 inches up on the side of a 10-inch springform pan.
3. Combine milk and caramels in a heavy-bottomed saucepan. Cook over medium heat until caramels are completely melted. Stir in chopped pecans. Cool slightly, then pour mixture onto the pie crust. Set aside.

4. Beat together the cream cheese, sugar and vanilla extract in large bowl using an electric mixer until blended.
5. Add eggs, one at a time, while mixing on low speed after each just until combined. Pour on top of caramel layer.
6. Bake in the oven for 1 hour 5 minutes to 1 hour 10 minutes or until center is almost set. Run a bread knife around the rim of pan to loosen cake. Allow to cool completely before removing the rim. Chill for 4 hours.
7. Drizzle with chocolate syrup and top with pecan halves. You can also top it with some whipped cream, if desired.
8. Serve and enjoy.

Nutritional Information:
Energy - 407 calories
Fat - 26.6 g
Carbohydrates - 38.1 g
Protein - 6.5 g
Sodium - 259 mg

Spiced Pumpkin Cheesecake

Preparation Time: 20 minutes
Total Time: 1 hour 45 minutes
Yield: 12 servings

Ingredients

1 ¼ cups (125 g) gingersnap biscuits, crushed

1/3 cup (85 g) butter, melted

2 (8 oz. or 250 g) cream cheese, at room temperature

1/2 cup (125 g) pumpkin puree

1 cup (300 g) condensed milk

1 Tbsp. (7 g) cornstarch

1/2 tsp. (1 g) cinnamon, ground

1/4 tsp. (0.5 g) nutmeg

3 (60 g) whole eggs

1/2 cup (125 g) all-purpose cream

Method

1. Preheat oven to 350 F.
2. In a large mixing bowl, combine crushed biscuits and butter. Mix well. Press the mixture onto the bottom of 10-inch springform pan. Bake for 10-12 minutes in the oven. Cool in wire rack. Set aside.
3. Using electric mixer, beat the cream cheese, pumpkin puree, condensed milk, cornstarch, cinnamon, and nutmeg until smooth. Add the eggs one at a time and the cream. Beat briefly just to combine. Pour the cream cheese filling mixture over the prepared crust.

4. Cover the bottom and sides of the springform pan with aluminium foil then place on water bath. Bake for 1 hour and 10 minutes or until tested done. Cool in wire rack.
5. Chill for at least 4 hours or until ready to serve.
6. Enjoy.

Nutritional Information:
Energy - 344 calories
Fat - 22.1 g
Carbohydrates - 25.9 g
Protein - 7.9 g
Sodium - 260 mg

Cherry Pie with Rhubarb and Honey

Preparation Time: 20 minutes
Total Time: 1 hour 20 minutes
Yield: 8 servings

Ingredients

1 (21 oz.) can cherry pie filling

2 cups chopped rhubarb

3/4 cup white sugar

2 1/2 tsp. quick-cooking tapioca

1 recipe pastry for double-crust pie (9-inch)

3 Tbsp. milk

Method

1. Preheat your oven to 400 F.
2. Combine the cherry pie filling, rhubarb, sugar, and tapioca in a large mixing bowl. Let sit for 15 minutes.
3. Pour filling onto unbaked pie shell, and cover with pie crust. Brush top with milk. Make some slits for air flow.
4. Bake in the oven for 40 to 45 minutes. Cool slightly before slicing.
5. Serve and enjoy.

Nutritional Information:

Energy - 249 calories

Fat - 5.3 g

Carbohydrates - 49.9 g

Protein - 1.4 g
Sodium - 118 mg

Carrot Cake with Prunes and Walnuts

Preparation Time: 15 minutes
Total Time: 40 minutes
Yield: 14 servings

Ingredients

2 cups all-purpose flour
1 cup white sugar
1 tsp. Kosher salt
2 tsp. cinnamon (ground)
1 tsp. baking soda
1/4 cup canola oil
1/4 cup applesauce
4 medium eggs
3 cups grated carrots
1 cup prunes (chopped)
1 cup walnuts (chopped)
1 (3 oz.) package cream cheese
1/4 cup heavy whipping cream
1 tsp. pure vanilla extract
2 cups sifted powdered sugar
1/2 cup walnuts (chopped)
cooking oil spray

Method

1. Preheat your oven to 350 F. Grease one 10-inch tube pan with oil spray.

2. Combine the flour, sugar, Kosher salt, cinnamon, soda, oil, and applesauce. Using an electric mixer, beat in the eggs one by one.
3. Then, fold in the carrots, prunes, and walnuts. Pour the batter mixture onto the prepared baking pan.
4. Bake at 350 F for 1 hour and 20 minutes. (Note: this cake can also be made in two 9-inch cake pans just reduce the baking time to 40 minutes) Allow the cake to cool in wire rack.
5. *To Make the Cream Cheese Frosting:* Using an electric mixer, whip the cream cheese and cream, then add the vanilla extract, and powdered sugar. Beat for 5 minutes or until smooth and fluffy.
6. Divide the cake and frosting to make 3 layers. Sprinkle with chopped walnuts.
7. Serve and enjoy.

Nutritional Information:

Energy - 391 calories

Fat - 16.2 g

Carbohydrates - 57.5 g

Protein - 7.6 g

Sodium - 311 mg

Baked Apples with Raisins and Pecans

Preparation Time: 10 minutes
Total Time: 40 minutes
Yield: 4 servings

Ingredients

4 large red delicious apple

1/4 cup brown sugar

1/2 cup seedless raisins

1/2 cup pecans (chopped)

2 Tbsp. butter (softened)

1 tsp. cinnamon (ground)

Method

1. Preheat your oven to 350 F.
2. Remove the core and seeds of apples, leaving about a 1/2-inch at the bottom.
3. Combine the brown sugar, raisins, pecans, butter, and cinnamon together in a bowl. Spoon mixture onto each apple. Place the stuffed apples in a large baking dish.
4. Bake in the oven for 30 minutes or until the apples are tender.
5. Transfer baked apples to individual plates and drizzle with pan juices.
6. Serve and enjoy.

Nutritional Information:

Energy - 309 calories
Fat - 11.6 g
Carbohydrates - 55.6 g
Protein - 2.1 g
Sodium - 47 mg

Crème Brulee Home-Style

Preparation Time: 10 minutes
Total Time: 2 hours 40 minutes
Yield: 4 servings

Ingredients
6 egg yolks
6 Tbsp. white sugar, divided
1/2 tsp. vanilla extract
2 1/2 cups all-purpose cream
2 Tbsp. brown sugar

Method
1. Preheat your oven to 300 F.
2. Whisk the egg yolks, 4 tablespoons white sugar, and vanilla extract in a medium mixing bowl, until it becomes thick and creamy.
3. Place cream into a saucepan and cook over low heat, stirring until it almost comes to boil. Immediately, remove the cream from heat.
4. Stir in cream into the egg yolk mixture and mix until combined well.
5. Pour the cream mixture into the top pan of a double boiler. Cook, stirring constantly over simmering water until the custard lightly coats the back of a spoon, about 3-4 minutes. Remove from heat immediately and pour into ramekins.
6. Place in the preheated oven and bake for about 30 minutes. Turn off the heat.

7. Put the ramekins to a wire rack and let cool. Keep refrigerated at least 2 hours or until ready to serve.
8. Preheat your broiler.
9. In a small bowl, mix together remaining 2 tablespoons white sugar and brown sugar. Sprinkle mixture evenly over custard.
10. Place the ramekins under broiler until sugar melts and browned, about 2 minutes. Watch carefully to prevent from burning.
11. Remove from heat and allow to cool. Chill until custard is set again.
12. Serve and enjoy.

Nutritional Information:
Energy - 263 calories
Fat - 15.1 g
Carbohydrates - 28.1 g
Protein - 5.2 g
Sodium - 62 mg

Blueberry Pecan Cheesecake in a Jar

Preparation Time: 30 minutes
Total Time: 30 minutes
Yield: 12 servings

Ingredients
1 ¼ cups sweet biscuits (crushed)
1/4 cup butter (melted)
1/4 cup brown sugar
1/2 cup pecan nuts (chopped)
2 (8-ounce) cream cheese
1 cup all-purpose cream
1/2 cup powdered sugar

Blueberry Sauce:
3 cups blueberries
1/2 cup raw sugar
1/4 cup water
2 Tbsp. lemon juice

You will need:
8 (6 oz.) mason jars with lid and rings

Method
1. *To Prepare the Sauce:* Combine the blueberries, sugar, water, and lemon juice in a medium saucepan. Bring to a boil. Reduce heat and cook until thick or to desired consistency. Remove from heat. Allow to cool.

2. In a mixing bowl, combine the biscuits, butter, brown sugar, and pecans. Mix well. Set aside.
3. Using electric mixer, beat the cream cheese until smooth. Reduce speed and add the cream and sugar, beating until well blended.
4. Spoon crust mixture and press onto the bottom of each mason jars. Top with cream cheese filling and blueberry sauce. Repeat procedure to make second layer. Cover tightly with lid. Place in the chiller for 4 to 6 hours or until ready to serve.

Nutritional Information:
Energy - 372 calories
Fat - 25.2 g
Carbohydrates - 32.5 g
Protein - 5.1 g
Sodium - 214 mg

Raspberry Kiwi and Pineapple Skewers

Preparation time: 10 minutes
Total time: 10 minutes
Yield: 20 servings

Ingredients

1 medium fresh pineapple (peeled and cored)

2 medium kiwifruit (peeled)

20 fresh raspberries

20 fresh mint leaves

20 toothpicks or decorative skewers

Method

1. Cut the pineapple and kiwifruit into cubes.
2. Thread 1 of each - raspberry, mint leaf, kiwi slice, and pineapple slice on each toothpick or skewer.
3. Place in a serving dish.
4. Serve and enjoy.

Nutritional Information:

Energy - 42 calories

Fat – 0.3 g

Carbohydrates – 10.5 g

Protein – 0.6 g

Sodium - 1 mg

Holiday Fruit Kebabs

Preparation Time: 10 minutes
Total Time: 10 minutes
Yield: 16 servings

Ingredients

2 medium peaches (peeled and stoned, and cut into 1-inch cubes)
2 medium kiwifruit (cut into 1-inch cubes)
2 cups of seedless watermelon (cut into 1-inch cubes)
1 cup blueberries
1 cup raspberries
Wooden skewers, to serve

Method

1. Thread the fruits alternately onto each skewer.
2. Place in a serving platter.
3. Serve and enjoy.

Nutritional Information:

Energy - 38 calories
Fat – 0.3 g
Carbohydrates – 9.2 g
Protein – 0.8 g
Sodium - 1 mg

Sugar-Coated Cranberries

Preparation Time: 5 minutes
Total Time: 2 hours 5 minutes
Yield: 24 servings

Ingredients
2 Tbsp. water
1 Tbsp. liquid egg substitute
1 (12 oz.) package fresh cranberries
1 cup granulated sugar

Method
1. In a medium bowl, mix together the water and liquid egg substitute until combined well. Coat the fresh cranberries with the mixture.
2. Spread out the granulated sugar on a baking sheet, and roll the cranberries in it until they are well coated.
3. Allow to dry at room temperature for about 2 hours.
4. Serve and enjoy.

Nutritional Information:
Energy - 39 calories
Fat - 0.0 g
Carbohydrates - 9.6 g
Protein - 0.1 g
Sodium - 1 mg

Pecan Tarts with Maple

Preparation Time: 15 minutes
Total Time: 1 hour 55 minutes
Yield: 48 servings

Ingredients

1 cup butter (softened)
1 (8 oz.) package cream cheese (softened)
2 1/4 cups all-purpose flour
4 whole eggs
2 cups packed brown sugar
1 cup maple syrup
1/4 cup butter (melted)
1/4 tsp. salt
1 tsp. pure vanilla extract
1 cup pecans (quartered)

Method

1. Using an electric mixer, whip the butter and cream cheese in a large bowl until smooth and fluffy.
2. Gradually, add the flour and mix thoroughly. Divide dough into 4 pieces and chill for at least an hour.
3. Meanwhile, combine the eggs, brown sugar, maple, butter, salt, vanilla extract, and pecans in a large bowl. Mix well and then set aside.
4. Preheat your oven to 350 F.
5. Cut each dough into 12 pieces, using a sharp knife. You should be able to get 48 pieces for the 4 dough.

Roll out each dough and lightly press into small muffin tins, covering all the way up to the edge.
6. Fill the tart shells with the prepared pecan mixture, up to 2/3 full only.
7. Bake for about 20-25 minutes or until lightly browned.
8. Remove from the oven and let them cool for 10 minutes.
9. Serve and enjoy.

Nutritional Information:
Energy - 136 calories
Fat - 7.9 g
Carbohydrates - 15.2 g
Protein - 1.6 g
Sodium - 67 mg

Homemade Port Cranberry Sauce

Preparation Time: 15 minutes
Total Time: 8 hours 30 minutes
Yield: 12 servings

Ingredients
1 (12 oz.) bag fresh cranberries
1/2 cup dark brown sugar (packed)
1/4 cup white sugar
1 large orange (juiced and zested)
1/2 cup port wine

Method
1. Combine the cranberries, brown sugar, white sugar, orange juice, zest, and port wine. Cook, stirring over medium-high flame until sugar has dissolved completely.
2. Lower the heat to medium-low and simmer for about 13-15 minutes, or until the cranberries have popped and the sauce has become thickened.
3. Allow the cranberry sauce to cool at room temperature and refrigerate overnight before serving.

Nutritional Information:
Energy - 69 calories
Fat - 0.0 g
Carbohydrates - 14.7 g
Protein - 0.2 g

Sodium - 2 mg

Christmas Hot Chocolate with Mallows

Preparation Time: 5 minutes
Total Time: 10 minutes
Yield: 4 servings

Ingredients

3 Tbsp. brown sugar
2 Tbsp. white sugar
1/4 cup cocoa powder (unsweetened)
1/8 tsp. cinnamon (ground)
1 pinch of salt
1/3 cup boiling water
3 cups whole milk
1 cup half-and-half cream (divided)
3/4 tsp. pure vanilla extract
small marshmallows

Method

1. Whisk brown sugar, white sugar, cocoa powder, cinnamon, and salt together in a saucepan. Pour boiling water. Mix until sugar is dissolved. Bring this mixture to a simmer over medium heat, stirring often.
2. Stir in milk and 1/2 cup half-and-half into the chocolate mixture. Cook and stir for about 2-3 minutes. Remove saucepan from heat. Stir in the remaining half-and-half cream and vanilla extract.
3. Divide hot chocolate among 4 mugs and top with marshmallows.

4. Serve and enjoy.

Nutritional Information:
Energy - 248 calories
Fat - 13.5 g
Carbohydrates - 25.7 g
Protein - 8.4 g
Sodium - 142 mg

Spiced Hot Chocolate with Nutella

Preparation Time: 5 minutes
Total Time: 10 minutes
Yield: 2 servings

Ingredients

1 (2 ounce) milk chocolate candy bar (chopped)

2 cups milk

2 Tbsp. Nutella

2 Tbsp. unsweetened cocoa powder

1/4 tsp. cinnamon (ground)

2 wafer sticks

Method

1. Place the chocolate pieces in a medium saucepan over medium-low heat.
2. Add milk and whisk constantly until the chocolate is melted, about 5 minutes.
3. Whisk in Nutella, cocoa powder, and cinnamon. Cook further 3-5 minutes, stirring often. Remove from heat. Pour into two mugs. Garnish with wafer stick.
4. Serve and enjoy.

Nutritional Information:

Energy - 368 calories

Fat - 18.6 g

Carbohydrates - 41.3 g

Protein - 12.1 g

Sodium - 145 mg

Hot Chocolate with Cinnamon

Preparation Time: 5 minutes
Total Time: 10 minutes
Yield: 4 servings

Ingredients

1/4 cup cocoa powder (unsweetened)

1/4 cup brown sugar

1/4 tsp. cinnamon (ground)

1 cup boiling water

1/4 cup melted semi-sweet chocolate

3 cups whole milk

4 cinnamon sticks

small marshmallows

Method

1. Combine the cocoa powder, sugar, and cinnamon together in a medium saucepan. Pour 1 cup boiling water. Mix well. Simmer over medium heat, stirring frequently.
2. Stir in melted chocolate, and milk. Cook, stirring for about 2-3 minutes more. Remove from heat.
3. Divide hot chocolate among 4 mugs, put 1 cinnamon stick, and top with marshmallows.
4. Serve and enjoy.

Nutritional Information:

Energy - 195 calories

Fat - 9.8 g
Carbohydrates - 27.5 g
Protein - 7.7 g
Sodium - 87 mg

Spiced Egg Nog

Preparation Time: 5 minutes
Total Time: 10 minutes
Yield: 3 servings

Ingredients
2 egg yolks
1/4 cup condensed milk
2 1/2 cups low-fat milk
1 tsp. pure vanilla extract
2 egg whites
1/4 tsp. nutmeg (ground)

Method
1. Beat egg yolks in a large mixing bowl, until they are thickened and light.
2. Whisk in condensed milk, low-fat milk, and vanilla extract.
3. In a separate small bowl, beat the egg whites until stiff, then add into the egg yolk-milk mixture. Mix well.
4. Divide among 3 cups. Sprinkle with nutmeg.
5. Serve and enjoy.

Nutritional Information:
Energy - 214 calories
Fat - 7.2 g

Carbohydrates - 24.2 g
Protein - 12.6 g
Sodium - 144 mg

Holiday Irish Coffee

Preparation Time: 5 minutes
Total Time: 5 minutes
Yield: 1 serving

Ingredients

1.5 fluid ounce Irish cream liqueur

3/4 cup hot brewed coffee

1/4 cup hot milk

a pinch of nutmeg (ground)

Method

1. Combine Irish cream, coffee, and hot milk in a coffee mug. Sprinkle with nutmeg.
2. Serve immediately and enjoy.

Nutritional Information:

Energy - 34 calories

Fat - 1.4 g

Carbohydrates - 3.1 g

Protein - 2.2 g

Sodium - 32 mg

Hot Apple Cider

Preparation Time: 5 minutes
Total Time: 15 minutes
Yield: 6 servings

Ingredients

6 cups apple cider
1/4 cup maple syrup
6 whole cloves
6 whole allspice berries
2 cinnamon sticks
1 orange peel (cut into thin strips)
1 lemon peel (cut into thin strips)

Method

1. Combine the apple cider and maple syrup in a large non-reactive saucepan.
2. Place the cloves, allspice berries, cinnamon sticks, orange peel, and lemon peel in the center of a clean cheesecloth (square). Get all the sides of the cheesecloth to enclose the spice bundle, then tie it up with a kitchen string. Then, add the spice bundle into the cider mixture.
3. Cook over medium heat for 5 to 10 minutes, or until the cider is heated through but not boiling.
4. Remove from heat and discard the spice bundle.
5. Divide cider among 6 cups. Garnish each cup with cinnamon stick and some sliced apples, if desired.
6. Serve and enjoy.

Nutritional Information:
Energy - 155 calories
Fat - 0.1 g
Carbohydrates - 37.0 g
Protein - 0.0 g
Sodium - 2 mg

Thanks a lot for reading!

I hope you enjoyed making the recipes here.

For more great tasting recipes, please check out all my published books on Amazon.